TO

_____

FROM

_____

DATE

_____

⁶Be careful for nothing; but in every thing by prayer and supplication with thanksgiving let your requests be made known unto God. ⁷And the peace of God, which passeth all understanding, shall keep your hearts and minds through Christ Jesus. Philippians 4:6-7

It's Your Turn to Pray

DR. SHARON FORDE-ATIKOSSIE

CITI OF
BOOKS

CITIOFBOOKS, INC.
3736 Eubank NE Suite A1
Albuquerque, NM 87111-3579
www.citiofbooks.com
Hotline: 1 (877) 389-2759
Fax: 1 (505) 930-7244

Ordering Information:
Quantity sales. Special discounts are available on quantity purchases by corporations, associations, and others. For details, contact the publisher at the address above.

Printed in the United States of America.

ISBN-13:	Softcover	979-8-89391-209-8
	eBook	979-8-89391-210-4

Library of Congress Control Number: 2024914306

IT IS YOUR TURN TO PRAY

Prayer works

Prayer Heals

Prayer Brings results

Prayer Brings knowledge

Pray brings Joy

Prayer brings peace of mind

Prayer Brings satisfaction.

Dear Reader,

I ask that you do not underestimate the power of prayer. God is mightier that you would ever know.

Always look to God for He is the author and finisher of your faith, seek Him for guidance in everything you do.

Listen to him; he speaks to you all the time.

Open your heart to him, and you will see what He will do for you.

He will Bless you bountifully.

Don't stop praying, and do not stop studying the Word of God!

Dr. Sharon Forde-Atikossie

IT IS YOUR TURN TO PRAY

As a young child growing up in my grandparents' household, I watched my cousins and aunts kneeling to pray each morning and evening. On Sundays, we would recite a Bible verse, explain what we learned in Sunday School, and sometimes repeat entire chapters from the Holy Bible.

The household rule was that everyone must recite the morning and evening prayers upon waking up and before going to bed.

It was fun for me because I had the opportunity to kneel with everyone, watching them pray and eagerly trying to be the first to recite the shortest Bible verses like "Jesus wept" or "Thou shall not steal" and to repeat Psalm 1. "Blessed is the man..." is something that has stuck with me for over fifty years.

THE MORNING PRAYER

When waking up: "Now I wake and see the light, God has kept me through the night, keep me safe, O Lord, I pray, keep and guide me through the day. Amen." After praying, everyone would say, "Good morning, Mother," and "Good morning, Daddy."

THE NIGHT PRAYER

"Now I lay me down to sleep, I pray the Lord my soul to keep. If I should die before I wake, I pray the Lord my soul to take. In my little bed I lie, Heavenly Father, hear my cry, Lord, protect me through this night, and bring me safe till morning light. Amen." After reciting this evening prayer, we would say, "Good night, Mother," and "Good night, Daddy."

This was the rule of our grandparents' home, and despite the fact that it was a rule that my grandfather put in place, the seed had been planted in each and every one of us.

I did not understand what we were doing, and it was great to hang out with the oldest sibling for at least a while, until they shew me away. I was praying to God for Him to bless me with wonderful things because we all were told by my grandparents that if we pray to God, He will answer our prayers. To me, this meant that everything we prayed for, we would get. So, I would pray and pray, believing that the harder I prayed, the more God would bless me. So I prayed harder, and so did the rest of the family.

As we all grew into adulthood, many of the family stopped praying because God did not give them what they asked for. I felt it was either our parents were lying to us, or God was playing games with us. Either way, no one was getting anything. This is what one may call a lack of knowledge. That is why it is very important for us to know and understand the Word of God, for nowhere in our prayers were we acknowledging God. We were busy telling Him what we wanted, as if we were demanding it and taking it for granted that we would get it. We were making petitions to God with selfish prayers, always wanting and demanding things for ourselves.

We could not even say thank you, God. That is why we need to know the Word of God, as the Bible says in 2 Timothy 2:15: "Study to show thyself approved unto God, a workman that needeth not to be ashamed, rightly dividing the word of truth."

WHAT IS PRAYER

According to Billy Graham, "Prayer is spiritual communication between man and God, a two-way relationship in which man should not only talk to God but also listen to Him. Prayer to God is like a child's conversation with his father. It is natural for a child to ask his father for the things he needs."

There are many promises in God's Word to encourage us to pray, such as: "He shall call upon me and I will answer him: I will be with him in trouble; I will deliver him, and honor him" (Psalm 91:15); "And it shall come to pass that before they call, I will answer; and while they are yet speaking, I will hear" (Isaiah 65:24); "Ask and it will be given to you; seek and you will find; knock and the door will be opened to you" (Matthew 7:7). The Scriptures tell us that we are to pray for one another and also assure us that God hears and answers prayers.

When you receive Christ into your heart, you become a child of God and have the privilege of talking to Him in prayer at any time about anything. The Christian life is a personal relationship with God through Jesus Christ. And best of all, it is a relationship that will last for all eternity.

There are things that one would want to know about prayers, such as:

Does God answer our prayers? YES. This is because God always wants us to bring our concerns to Him, and He has promised to answer us. He does not only hear us; He is willing and always ready to respond to us. (Psalm 55:16-17: "As for me, I call to God, and the LORD saves me. Evening, morning, and noon I cry out in distress, and He hears my voice.")

Does God hear our prayers? The Bible tells us that God hears our prayers - 2 Chronicles 7:14: "If My people who are called by My name humble themselves, pray and seek My face, and turn from their evil ways, then I will hear from heaven, forgive their sin, and heal their land."

John 9:31: "We know that God does not listen to sinners, but if anyone is a worshiper of God and does His will, God listens to him."

Isaiah 65:24: "Before they call I will answer; while they are yet speaking, I will hear."

Psalm 66:19: "But truly God has listened; He has attended to the voice of my prayer."

1 John 5:14-15: "And this is the confidence that we have before Him: If we ask anything according to His will, He hears us."

WHAT IS THE IMPORTANCE OF PRAYER

The Bible says it best - 1 John 5:14-15: "This is the confidence we have in approaching God: that if we ask anything according to His will, He hears us. And if we know that He hears us—whatever we ask—we know that we have what we asked of Him."

I learned that the Bible encourages us to be confident that God hears our prayer. It states that "This is the confidence we have in approaching God: that if we ask anything according to His will, He hears us. And if we know that He hears us, whatever we ask, we know that we have what we asked of Him."

When we pray, we enjoy God.

One who does not believe in God does not pray or believe in prayer. As a child of God, you must have faith and believe that there is a true and living God that we must serve. We must pray to Him in spirit and in truth, and have the faith and belief that God will answer our prayers, for I learned that it is a pathway to joy. Having a relationship with God brings us peace and joy, which shows that we are having a relationship with Him, our Father.

When we pray, we experience peace, for it is a pathway to joy. It is impossible to talk to our Father and listen to God and not experience it. In the Old Testament times, prayer and joy came hand in hand in His "house of prayer." God said of foreigners who bind themselves to Him, "... these I will bring to my holy mountain and give them joy in my house of prayer" (Isaiah 56:6-7). Because of Jesus dying on the cross for us, we do not have to go to any house of prayer; we can experience the same joy in prayer anytime and anywhere.

HOW TO PRAY

We pray in the Holy Spirit.

Find a quiet place where you feel comfortable and address God by name, such as Father in Heaven or Heavenly Father.

Speak from your heart and share your hopes and desires as well as your worries and problems with God. Pray with love and grief, with delight and thanksgiving, but also with authentic repentance and sincerity.

End your prayer by saying "in the name of Jesus Christ, amen" or something similar. This shows your respect and gratitude for Jesus Christ, who is the mediator between you and God.

DAY 1
MORNING PRAYER

Heavenly Father, I bless Your holy name. Thank You for waking me up this morning. I glorify Your name, Lord. Thank You for the gift of life that You have given to me this day. I praise Your holy name, Lord. Please guide my mind and footsteps so that I can accomplish all tasks at hand. In Jesus' name, Amen.

"Enter His gates with thanksgiving and His courts with praise; give thanks to Him and praise His name." (Psalm 100:4)

"Do not be anxious about anything, but in every situation, by prayer and petition, with thanksgiving, present your requests to God." (Philippians 4:6)

"Give thanks to the Lord, for He is good; His love endures forever." (Psalm 107:1)

"Let the peace of Christ rule in your hearts, since as members of one body you were called to peace. And be thankful." (Colossians 3:15)

DAY 1
MY MORNING PRAYER

_____

_____

_____

_____

_____

_____

_____

_____

_____

_____

_____

_____

_____

_____

_____

_____

_____

DAY 1
EVENING PRAYER

God, I thank you for guiding my footsteps through the day and keeping me safe. You are awesome to me not only today, but always. Thank you for going before me during the day, and I glorify and magnify your name because you are worthy to be praised. Please bless me to have a good night. In Jesus' name, Amen.

"Give thanks to the Lord, for he is good; his love endures forever." (Psalm 107:1)

"Let the peace of Christ rule in your hearts, since as members of one body you were called to peace. And be thankful." (Colossians 3:15)

DAY 1
MY EVENING PRAYER

_____

_____

_____

_____

_____

_____

_____

_____

_____

_____

_____

_____

_____

_____

_____

_____

_____

DAY 2
MORNING PRAYER

Lord, this is a new day. I offer this day to you, Lord. May everything I do today be done decently and in order, with love and for your glory. Please guide my thoughts, my words, and my actions, and help me to be a source of kindness and encouragement to others. In Jesus' name, Amen.

"Call to me and I will answer you and tell you great and unsearchable things you do not know." (Jeremiah 33:3)

"Those who trust in themselves are fools, but those who walk in wisdom are kept safe." (Proverbs 28:26)

"Above all else, guard your heart, for everything you do flows from it." (Proverbs 4:23)

DAY 2
MY MORNING PRAYER

_____

_____

_____

_____

_____

_____

_____

_____

_____

_____

_____

_____

_____

_____

_____

_____

DAY 2
EVENING PRAYER

Among all things, Lord, you have blessed me with today, so I glorify you. You have given me the precious gift of life, and I am grateful to receive it. You have shown me love, you have brought me through the day, and I pray that you continue to bless me and guide me through the night. I will give thanks to you, LORD, because of your righteousness that you clothe me with. In Jesus' name, Amen.

"I will sing the praises of the name of the LORD Most High." (Psalm 7:17)

"Give thanks in all circumstances; for this is God's will for you in Christ Jesus." (1 Thessalonians 5:18)

DAY 2
MY EVENING PRAYER

_____

_____

_____

_____

_____

_____

_____

_____

_____

_____

_____

_____

_____

_____

_____

_____

_____

_____

DAY 3
MORNING PRAYER

Dear Lord, thank you for the gift of life that you bless me with. I am grateful for the blessings of life, health, and the opportunity to serve you, my God. Please guide my thoughts, words, and actions today, and may everything I do be in accordance with Your will. In Jesus' name, I pray. Amen.

"Be very careful, then, how you live—not as unwise but as wise, making the most of every opportunity, because the days are evil." (Ephesians 5:15-16)

"The LORD is my shepherd, I lack nothing." (Psalm 23:1)

"Whoever pursues righteousness and love finds life, prosperity, and honor." (Proverbs 21:21)

DAY 3
MY MORNING PRAYER

_____

_____

_____

_____

_____

_____

_____

_____

_____

_____

_____

_____

_____

_____

_____

_____

_____

_____

DAY 3
EVENING PRAYER

Dear Lord, I praise your Holy name. I give grace and glory unto you for you are the author and finisher of my faith. I am grateful for the blessings of my life. Peace be unto you.

Thank you for the guidance, the strength, and health.

In Jesus' name, I pray Amen

And God is able to bless you abundantly, so that in all things at all times, having all that you need, you will abound in every good work. (2 Corinthians 9:8)

He has saved us and called us to a holy life—not because of anything we have done but because of his own purpose and grace. This grace was given us in Christ Jesus before the beginning of time." (2 Timothy 1:9)

But those who hope in the LORD will renew their strength. They will soar on wings like eagles; they will run and not grow weary, they will walk and not be faint." (Isaiah 40:31)

DAY 3
MY EVENING PRAYER

_____

_____

_____

_____

_____

_____

_____

_____

_____

_____

_____

_____

_____

_____

_____

_____

_____

_____

_____

DAY 4
MORNING PRAYER

A Prayer for Strength and Guidance: Heavenly Father, as I begin this day, I ask for Your strength and guidance. Help me to face the challenges ahead with courage and grace. May Your Holy Spirit be my constant companion, leading me in the path of righteousness. In Jesus' name, I pray. Amen.

"And God is able to bless you abundantly, so that in all things at all times, having all that you need, you will abound in every good work." (2 Corinthians 9:8)

"He has saved us and called us to a holy life—not because of anything we have done but because of his own purpose and grace. This grace was given us in Christ Jesus before the beginning of time." (2 Timothy 1:9)

"But those who hope in the LORD will renew their strength. They will soar on wings like eagles; they will run and not grow weary, they will walk and not be faint." (Isaiah 40:31)

DAY 4
MY MORNING PRAYER

_____

_____

_____

_____

_____

_____

_____

_____

_____

_____

_____

_____

_____

_____

_____

_____

DAY 4
EVENING PRAYER

Lord, I thank you. Lord, I give you praise and glory because it belongs to you. Thank you for guiding me through the day. Thank you, Holy Spirit. I bless your name for the strength and guidance that you have given me. Thank you for the courage and strength, and thank you for placing the cloth of righteousness upon me. In Jesus' name, I pray. Amen.

"So do not fear, for I am with you; do not be dismayed, for I am your God. I will strengthen you and help you; I will uphold you with my righteous right hand." (Isaiah 41:10)

"Have I not commanded you? Be strong and courageous. Do not be afraid; do not be discouraged, for the Lord your God will be with you wherever you go." (Joshua 1:9)

DAY 4
MY EVENING PRAYER

_____

_____

_____

_____

_____

_____

_____

_____

_____

_____

_____

_____

_____

_____

_____

_____

_____

_____

DAY 5
MORNING PRAYER

Lord Jesus, you woke me up this day. Grant me your peace this morning, and help me to let go of worry and anxiety that may come in my path this day. Lord, I know that you are in control of my life. Please fill my heart with joy and peace, and grant me the boldness to use wisdom. Fill my heart with joy and direct my path today, tomorrow, and always. In Jesus' name, Amen.

"Let the peace of Christ rule in your hearts, since as members of one body you were called to peace. And be thankful." (Colossians 3:15)

"Peace I leave with you; my peace I give you. I do not give to you as the world gives. ... In this world you will have trouble. But take heart! I have overcome the world." (John 16:33)

"You will keep in perfect peace those whose minds are steadfast, because they trust in you." (Isaiah 26:3)

DAY 5
MY MORNING PRAYER

_____

_____

_____

_____

_____

_____

_____

_____

_____

_____

_____

_____

_____

_____

_____

_____

_____

DAY 5
EVENING PRAYER

Prince of Peace, Lord of Hosts, thank you for guiding me through this day. I come before you with a heart full of joy and peace. I ask that you continue to grant me the inner peace that surpasses all understanding. Calm the storms within me and fill me with the assurance of your presence. Help me to cast my anxieties upon you and to trust in your perfect peace. In Jesus' name, I pray. Amen.

"Teach me Your way, O Lord, And lead me in a level path Because of my foes." (Psalm 27:11)

"For You are my rock and my fortress; For Your name's sake You will lead me and guide me." (Psalm 31:3)

"For the choir director; on a stringed instrument. A Psalm of David. Hear my cry, O God; Give heed to my prayer. From the end of the earth I call to You when my heart is faint; Lead me to the rock that is higher than I." (Psalm 61:1-2)

DAY 5
MY EVENING PRAYER

_____

_____

_____

_____

_____

_____

_____

_____

_____

_____

_____

_____

_____

_____

_____

_____

_____

DAY 6
MORNING PRAYER

O God, my Father, my Creator, my Sustainer of Heaven and Earth. Thank you for waking me up this day, and blessing me with this gift of life. You are the Lord of Hosts, and the King of Kings. Help me to put on the cloth of righteousness. Use me as an instrument of Your love and grace, and help me to be a blessing to others around me. Let your light shine upon me always, so that I can be an instrument of Your love and draw Your children to You. You said you would never leave me nor forsake me, and I thank you for Your love and kindness. May my life be a testimony today and always for Your glory. In the name of Jesus, I pray. Amen.

"For this boy I prayed, and the Lord has given me my petition which I asked of Him." (1 Samuel 1:27)

"At that time the Feast of the Dedication took place at Jerusalem." (John 10:22)

"The leaders offered the dedication offering for the altar when it was anointed, so the leaders offered their offering before the altar." (Numbers 7:10)

DAY 6
MY MORNING PRAYER

_____

_____

_____

_____

_____

_____

_____

_____

_____

_____

_____

_____

_____

_____

_____

_____

_____

DAY 6
EVENING PRAYER

Heavenly Father, you are the author and finisher of my faith. Thank you for your mercy and grace. Thank you for keeping me through the day. Thank you for your love and kindness. Forgive me of my sins and shortcomings, and guide me through the night, and keep me safe.

"In peace I will lie down and sleep, for you alone, LORD, make me dwell in safety." (Psalm 4:8)

"O continue Your lovingkindness to those who know You, And Your righteousness to the upright in heart." (Psalm 36:10)

"Because Your lovingkindness is better than life, My lips will praise You." (Psalm 63:3)

"Let the one who is wise heed these things, and ponder the loving deeds of the LORD." (Psalm 107:43)

DAY 6
MY EVENING PRAYER

_____

_____

_____

_____

_____

_____

_____

_____

_____

_____

_____

_____

_____

_____

_____

_____

_____

_____

DAY 7
MORNING PRAYER

Thank you for a new day. Thank you for your compassion and for renewing my spirit this morning. Great is your faithfulness and your steadfast love that you give to me. O Lord! I don't know what all is going to happen today and how much I'll get done, but you do, so please forgive me of my sins, and give me the strength to endure. With this, I pray. In Jesus' name, Amen.

"Therefore, confess your sins to one another and pray for one another, that you may be healed. The prayer of a righteous person has great power as it is working." (James 5:16)

"He has delivered us from the domain of darkness and transferred us to the kingdom of his beloved Son, in whom we have redemption, the forgiveness of sins." (Colossians 1:13-14)

"Be kind to one another, tenderhearted, forgiving one another, as God in Christ forgave you." (Ephesians 4:32)

DAY 7
MORNING PRAYER

_____

_____

_____

_____

_____

_____

_____

_____

_____

_____

_____

_____

_____

_____

_____

_____

_____

_____

DAY 7
EVENING PRAYER

O Lord our God, I praise your holy name this evening. Thank you for blessing me. Thank you for believing in me this day. I glorify your name. Please, Lord, keep me and my family in peace during this night and at all times. Keep our hearts and minds whole. Keep my thoughts secure in the holy name of Jesus so that I may be protected at all times from the snares of the enemy. Let me offer blessing and glory to you, our Father, and to the Son, Jesus. Amen.

"May he give you the desire of your heart and make all your plans succeed." (Psalm 20:4)

"Commit to the Lord whatever you do, and he will establish your plans." (Proverbs 16:3)

"For I know the plans I have for you, declares the Lord, plans to prosper you and not to harm you, plans to give you hope and a future." (Jeremiah 29:11)

DAY 7
MY EVENING PRAYER

_____

_____

_____

_____

_____

_____

_____

_____

_____

_____

_____

_____

_____

_____

_____

_____

_____

_____

DAY 8
MORNING PRAYER

Thank you, God, for waking me up. Fill me with Your Holy Spirit, and give me the strength to go through this day. Grant me mercy upon my soul, oh God, and awaken me to the wonder of Your salvation, and quicken my spirit to the reality of Your work in my life. I admit that I am a sinner. I have done many things that don't please you. I have lived my life for myself only. I ask you to take control of my life, and help me to live every day for you. I love you, Lord, and I thank you that I will spend all eternity with you. In Jesus' name, Amen.

"Little children, let us not love in word or talk but in deed and in truth." (1 John 3:18)

"For our boast is this, the testimony of our conscience, that we behaved in the world with simplicity and godly sincerity, not by earthly wisdom but by the grace of God, and supremely so toward you." (2 Corinthians 1:12)

"In all things showing thyself a pattern

of good works: in doctrine showing uncorruptness, gravity, sincerity." (Titus 2:7)

"Now therefore fear the Lord and serve him in sincerity and in faithfulness. Put away the gods that your fathers served beyond the River and in Egypt, and serve the Lord." (Joshua 24:14

DAY 8
MY MORNING PRAYER

_____

_____

_____

_____

_____

_____

_____

_____

_____

_____

_____

_____

_____

_____

_____

_____

_____

_____

DAY 8
EVENING PRAYER

Heavenly Father, please grant me a good night's sleep tonight so that I can awake in the morning refreshed and ready to begin another day of loving you. Thank you again for blessings so undeserved and too numerous to count. I love you, Lord, and thank you for allowing me to be your child, even though I am not worthy. Let the morning bring me word of your unfailing love, for I have put my trust in you. Show me the way I should go, for to you I entrust my life. In Jesus' name, Amen.

"Let the morning bring me word of your unfailing love, for I have put my trust in you. Show me the way I should go, for to you I entrust my life." (Psalm 143:8)

"And over all these virtues put on love, which binds them all together in perfect unity." (Colossians 3:14)

"Let not steadfast love and faithfulness forsake you; bind them around your neck; write them on the tablet of your heart. So you will find favor and good success in the sight of God and man." (Proverbs 3:3-4)

DAY 8
MY EVENING PRAYER

_____

_____

_____

_____

_____

_____

_____

_____

_____

_____

_____

_____

_____

_____

_____

_____

_____

_____

DAY 9
MORNING PRAYER

Lord, I thank you for waking me up today. I know that you have a purpose for me, and my mind is filled with joy. Create in me a clean heart, and give me the strength to endure. Let your Holy Spirit pour into me so that I can live for you daily. Cleanse me, Lord, guide me, and protect me in everything that I do. I bless your holy name. In Jesus' name, Amen.

"Create in me a clean heart, O God, and renew a right spirit within me." (Psalm 51:10)

"I will sprinkle clean water on you, and you shall be clean from all your uncleannesses, and from all your idols I will cleanse you. And I will give you a new heart, and a new spirit I will put within you. And I will remove the heart of stone from your flesh and give you a heart of flesh. And I will put my Spirit within you, and cause you to walk in my statutes and be careful to obey my rules." (Ezekiel 36:25-27)

"And he made no distinction between us and them, having cleansed their hearts by faith." (Acts 15:9

DAY 9
MY MORNING PRAYER

_____

_____

_____

_____

_____

_____

_____

_____

_____

_____

_____

_____

_____

_____

_____

_____

_____

_____

_____

DAY 9
EVENING PRAYER

I sing a joyful song unto you, my God, my Father, for you are the author and finisher of our faith. You are worthy to be praised. Thank you in advance for beating back the enemy. Although life is full of challenges, I choose to believe and trust in you. I surrender my all to you tonight, and I choose to rest in the warmth of your embrace. Thank you for guiding my steps today. In Jesus' name, Amen.

"Trust in the LORD with all your heart and lean not on your own understanding." (Proverbs 3:5)

"But blessed is the one who trusts in the LORD, whose confidence is in him." (Jeremiah 17:7)

"When I am afraid, I put my trust in you." (Psalm 56:3)

"Commit to the LORD whatever you do, and he will establish your plans." (Proverbs 16:3)

DAY 9
MY EVENING PRAYERS

_____

_____

_____

_____

_____

_____

_____

_____

_____

_____

_____

_____

_____

_____

_____

_____

_____

DAY 10
MORNING PRAYER

Thank God for your righteousness. Thank God for your blessings. Thank God for life. Thank God for joy. Thank God for peace. Thank God for endurance. You are the greatest, Lord. You are the potter, and I am the clay. I am so thankful you are God, and the gospel is true, and you are my helper, redeemer, and my God. Amen, I pray, in Jesus' name.

"We adore you as the one who is over all things. Wealth and honor come from you alone, for you rule over everything. Power and might are in your hand, and at your discretion, people are made great and given strength." (1 Chronicles 29:11-12, NLT)

"Remember the former things, those of long ago; I am God, and there is no other; I am God, and there is none like me. I make known the end from the beginning, from ancient times, what is still to come. I say, 'My purpose will stand, and I will do all that I please.'" (Isaiah 46:9-10, NIV)

DAY 10
MY MORNING PRAYER

_____

_____

_____

_____

_____

_____

_____

_____

_____

_____

_____

_____

_____

_____

_____

_____

_____

_____

DAY 10
EVENING PRAYER

Almighty God, we bless you in my life. We give you all the praise and glory. We thank you for your faithfulness, even though I am not always faithful to you. Lord Jesus, I ask you to give me all-around peace in my mind, body, soul, and spirit. We want you to heal and remove everything that is causing stress, grief, and sorrow in our lives, and please guide our path through life and make our enemies be at peace with us. Lord, let your peace reign in my family. In Jesus' name, Amen.

"I charge you in the presence of God and of Christ Jesus, who is to judge the living and the dead, and by his appearing and his kingdom: preach the word; be ready in season and out of season; reprove, rebuke, and exhort, with complete patience and teaching. For the time is coming when people will not endure sound teaching, but having itching ears they will accumulate for themselves teachers to suit their own passions, and will turn away from listening to the truth and wander off into myths. As for you, always be sober-minded, endure suffering, do the work of an evangelist, fulfill your ministry." (2 Timothy 4:1-22)

"Children, obey your parents in the Lord, for this is right. 'Honor your father and mother' (this is the first commandment with a promise), 'that it may go well with you and that you may live long in the land.'" (Ephesians 6:1-3)

"Do you not know that you are God's temple and that God's Spirit dwells in you?" (1 Corinthians 3:16)

DAY 10
MY EVENING PRAYER

_____

_____

_____

_____

_____

_____

_____

_____

_____

_____

_____

_____

_____

_____

_____

_____

_____

DAY 11
MORNING PRAYER

Heavenly Father, we bless your holy name. You are the God of my life and my salvation. I welcome another new day so that I can glorify you. Thank you for this gift of life that you bless me with. I thank you for the sleep that has refreshed me. I thank you for this chance to make a new beginning. This day, Lord, is full of promise and opportunity. Show me what to do so that I can accomplish my tasks today in an orderly manner. Keep me from any word that would hurt, belittle, or destroy, and may the thoughts of my mind be pleasing in your sight. In Jesus' name, Amen.

"For I know the plans I have for you, declares the Lord, plans to prosper you and not to harm you, plans to give you hope and a future." (Jeremiah 29:11)

DAY 11
MY MORNING PRAYER

_____

_____

_____

_____

_____

_____

_____

_____

_____

_____

_____

_____

_____

_____

_____

_____

_____

_____

DAY 11
EVENING PRAYER

Father, I can barely lift my eyes to you. It's all I can do to cry out for help. Please extend your grace to me this day.

Help me to see that you are in this and that you are with me. Help me to remember that you are not surprised or taken off guard by the events of this day. Forgive me for my fears about this day.

Forgive me for how I have complained and muttered about how hard this day has been.

Forgive me for forgetting that you are with me. Forgive me for forgetting who I am because of what your Son, Jesus Christ, has done.

Forgive me for failing to remember the glorious truths and riches I have because of the gospel.

Father, hear my prayer. Grant me gospel hope in the midst of this hard day. Help me to cling to your grace, your wisdom, and your strength.

DAY 11
MY EVENING PRAYER

DAY 12
MORNING PRAYER

Dear God, thank you for your amazing power and work in our lives. Thank you for your goodness and for your blessings over us. Thank you for your great love and care. Thank you for your sacrifice so that I might have freedom and life. Forgive me when I don't thank you enough for who you are, for all you do, and for all you've given. Help me to set my eyes and my heart on you afresh. Renew my spirit, and fill me with your peace and joy. We love you, and we need you this day and every day. We give you praise and thanks, for you alone are worthy! In Jesus' name, Amen.

"'I have the right to do anything,' you say—but not everything is beneficial. 'I have the right to do anything'—but I will not be mastered by anything." (1 Corinthians 6:12)

"But Scripture has locked up everything under the control of sin, so that what was promised, being given through faith in Jesus Christ, might be given to those who believe." (Galatians 3:22)

"When hard pressed, I cried to the LORD; he brought me into a spacious place." (Psalm 118:5)

DAY 12
MY MORNING PRAYER

_____

_____

_____

_____

_____

_____

_____

_____

_____

_____

_____

_____

_____

_____

_____

_____

_____

_____

DAY 12
EVENING PRAYER

Heavenly Father, as I am ready to go to bed, I bless your holy name. I ask that you bless me through the night. You have helped me with guidance and direction today so that I was able to accomplish all my tasks. Help me to be more like you. Touch my body from the crown of my head to the soles of my feet. I ask that you protect me and keep me safe from all harm, seen and unseen, and grant me peace of mind. Trust your plan that you have for me. In Jesus' name, Amen.

"Rescue the weak and the needy; deliver them from the hand of the wicked." (Psalm 82:4)

"Let each of you look not only to his own interests, but also to the interests of others." (Philippians 2:4)

"Rescue those who are being taken away to death; hold back those who are stumbling to the slaughter." (Proverbs 24:11)

"Beloved, never avenge yourselves, but leave it to the wrath of God, for it is written,

'Vengeance is mine, I will repay,' says the Lord." (Romans 12:19)

"Above all, keep loving one another earnestly, since love covers a multitude of sins." (1 Peter 4:8)

DAY 12
MY EVENING PRAYER

_____

_____

_____

_____

_____

_____

_____

_____

_____

_____

_____

_____

_____

_____

_____

_____

_____

_____

DAY 13
MORNING PRAYER

Thank you, Jesus, for the day. Thank you, Lord, for waking me up. I bless your holy name. Go before me, God, and grant me the favor to be safe. Give me the strength to live for you, and keep me safe as I walk this road. I seek strength, wisdom, and guidance as I face the challenges of life. Help me to always be there for each other and to support one another. Help me to forgive one another and to always be kind and compassionate. In Jesus' name, Amen.

"I will have mercy on whom I will have mercy, and I will have compassion on whom I will have compassion." (Exodus 33:19)

"Praise be to the God and Father of our Lord Jesus Christ, the Father of compassion and the God of all comfort, who comforts us in all our troubles, so that we can comfort those in any trouble with the comfort we ourselves receive from God." (2 Corinthians 1:3-4)

"Therefore if you have any encouragement from being united with Christ, if any comfort from his love, if any common sharing in the Spirit, if any tenderness and compassion, then make my joy complete by being like-minded, having the same love, being one in spirit and of one mind." (Philippians 2:1-2)

DAY 13
MY MORNING PRAYER

_____

_____

_____

_____

_____

_____

_____

_____

_____

_____

_____

_____

_____

_____

_____

_____

_____

_____

_____

DAY 13
EVENING PRAYER

To God be the glory. Thank you for blessing this day. I admit that I sometimes forget you are with me; please forgive me for that. I need to get to know you better. Help me to put you first in every area of my life. Help me to live one day at a time, and help me not to worry about tomorrow but instead focus on what you're doing in my life right now. I trust in your promise to take care of every one of my needs, including financial, relational, physical, social, spiritual, and emotional. Keep me this night from all harm and danger, seen and unseen. In Jesus' name, Amen.

"Rescue the weak and the needy; deliver them from the hand of the wicked." (Psalm 82:4)

"Let each of you look not only to his own interests, but also to the interests of others." (Philippians 2:4)

"Rescue those who are being taken away to death; hold back those who are stumbling to the slaughter." (Proverbs 24:11)

"Beloved, never avenge yourselves, but leave it to the wrath of God, for it is written, 'Vengeance is mine, I will repay,' says the Lord." (Romans 12:19)

DAY 13
MY EVENING PRAYER

_____

_____

_____

_____

_____

_____

_____

_____

_____

_____

_____

_____

_____

_____

_____

_____

_____

_____

DAY 14
MORNING PRAYER

Dear God, I come before you this morning, as the day breaks. I bless your holy name and thank you for allowing me to see another day. May your joy shine through me, Lord. I come before you, O Lord, and drink in this moment of peace, that I may carry something of your hope, love, and joy today in my heart. Allow my heart not to be filled with chaos and confusion. I am asking you for strength and peace that only you can give me. Let your Holy Spirit flow through me in spirit and truth. In Jesus' name, Amen.

"May the God of hope fill you with all joy and peace in believing, so that by the power of the Holy Spirit you may abound in hope." (Romans 15:13)

"Rejoice in hope, be patient in tribulation, be constant in prayer." (Romans 12:12)

"Rejoice in the Lord always; again I will say, rejoice." (Philippians 4:4)

"Count it all joy, my brothers, when you meet trials of various kinds." (James 1:2)

"But the fruit of the Spirit is love, joy, peace, patience, kindness, goodness, faithfulness." (Galatians 5:22)

DAY 14
MY MORNING PRAYER

_____

_____

_____

_____

_____

_____

_____

_____

_____

_____

_____

_____

_____

_____

_____

_____

_____

_____

DAY 14
EVENING PAYER

To God be the glory, great things He has done. Thank you for blessing me through this day. You know my heart and mind. I pray that tomorrow I would stand in your perfect will for my life. Help me to make prayerful decisions that will bring glory to you. Watch over me, my God, and keep me safe wherever I go. I pray that I would be productive and use the gifts and skills you have given me. I ask that you help me have patience with those I encounter and extend grace when it is needed. I am grateful that you are in control. I place tomorrow in your hands and thank you for blessing me and keeping me safe. In Jesus' name, Amen.

"Therefore no one will be declared righteous in God's sight by the works of the law; rather, through the law we become conscious of our sin." (Romans 3:20)

"But now apart from the law the righteousness of God has been made known, to which the Law and the Prophets testify." (Romans 3:21)

"This righteousness is given through faith in Jesus Christ to all who believe. There is no difference between Jew and Gentile." (Romans 3:22)

"For all have sinned and fall short of the glory of God." (Romans 3:23)

"And all are justified freely by his grace through the redemption that came by Christ Jesus." (Romans 3:24)

DAY 14
MY EVENING PRAYER

_____

_____

_____

_____

_____

_____

_____

_____

_____

_____

_____

_____

_____

_____

_____

_____

_____

_____

DAY 15
MORNING PRAYER

God, we give you sincere thanks for the rest of the past night and the gift of a new day, with its opportunities to serve you today, tomorrow, and forever.

Grant that we may so pass its hours in the perfect freedom of your service, that in the evening, we may again give you thanks; through Jesus Christ our Lord. Amen.

"No weapon that is fashioned against you shall succeed, and you shall refute every tongue that rises against you in judgment. This is the heritage of the servants of the Lord and their vindication from me, declares the Lord." (Isaiah 54:17)

DAY 15
MY MORNING PRAYER

_____

_____

_____

_____

_____

_____

_____

_____

_____

_____

_____

_____

_____

_____

_____

_____

_____

_____

DAY 15
EVENING PRAYER

Holy Spirit, please encircle me, come hold me safe and secure tonight. Please wrap your arms around me, and wrap my mind with your truth. Guide my thoughts and calm my fears. Steady my emotions, Lord, that you would guide my feelings. May I not be overcome by upset. Sustain my soul with a vision for the future and hope for tomorrow. I need you. Amen.

"Who is like the wise? And who knows the interpretation of a thing? A man's wisdom makes his face shine, and the hardness of his face is changed. I say: Keep the king's command, because of God's oath to him. Be not hasty to go from his presence. Do not take your stand in an evil cause, for he does whatever he pleases. For the word of the king is supreme, and who may say to him, 'What are you doing?' Whoever keeps a command will know no evil thing, and the wise heart will know the proper time and the just way." (Ecclesiastes 8:1-5)

"So Jesus also suffered outside the gate in

order to sanctify the people through his own blood." (Hebrews 13:12)

"But we have this treasure in jars of clay, to show that the surpassing power belongs to God and not to us." (2 Corinthians 4:7)

DAY 15
MY EVENING PRAYER

_____

_____

_____

_____

_____

_____

_____

_____

_____

_____

_____

_____

_____

_____

_____

_____

_____

_____

DAY 16
MORNING PRAYER

Morning prayers for protection help us remember that God's providence is always present and omnipresent. Nothing is more powerful than God, and nothing happens without God allowing it. When we pray for God's protection, we show faith in Him and submission to His will. Blessed are those who seek shelter in God, who grants the faithful eternal safeguard in His Kingdom.

"*He who dwells in the shelter of the Most High will abide in the shadow of the Almighty. I will say to the Lord, 'My refuge and my fortress, my God, in whom I trust.'*" (Psalm 91:1-2)

"No weapon that is fashioned against you shall succeed, and you shall refute every tongue that rises against you in judgment. This is the heritage of the servants of the LORD and their vindication from me, declares the LORD." (Isaiah 54:17)

"God is our refuge and strength, a very present help in trouble." (Psalm 46:1)

"Be strong and courageous. Do not fear or

be in dread of them, for it is the LORD your God who goes with you. He will not leave you or forsake you." (Deuteronomy 31:6)

"But the Lord is faithful. He will establish you and guard you against the evil one." (2 Thessalonians 3:3)

DAY 16
MY MORNING PRAYER

_____

_____

_____

_____

_____

_____

_____

_____

_____

_____

_____

_____

_____

_____

_____

_____

_____

_____

_____

DAY 16
EVENING PRAYER

O Lord God Almighty, as You have taught us to call the evening, the morning, and the noonday one day; and have made the sun to know its going down: Dispel the darkness of our hearts, that by Your brightness we may know You to be the true God and eternal light, living and reigning forever and ever. Amen.

"I am the Alpha and the Omega," says the Lord God, "who is and who was and who is to come, the Almighty." (Revelation 1:8)

"For the wages of sin is death, but the free gift of God is eternal life in Christ Jesus our Lord." (Romans 6:23)

"Before the mountains were brought forth, or ever you had formed the earth and the world, from everlasting to everlasting you are God." (Psalm 90:2)

"For God so loved the world, that he gave his only Son, that whoever believes in him should not perish but have eternal life." (John 3:16)

DAY 16
MY EVENING PRAYER

_____

_____

_____

_____

_____

_____

_____

_____

_____

_____

_____

_____

_____

_____

_____

_____

_____

DAY 17
MORNING PRAYER

O Lord, our redemption. Be our protection. Direct my mind by your gracious presence, and watch over my paths. Guide me with your love through the hidden snares of life. Fix my heart on you as I go forward through the day. Lead me to the path of righteousness, and show me what to do so I cannot fail you. I thank you for your blessing and grace. Thank you for staying in the driver's seat of my life. Allow me to have the faith and belief that you are the true and living God that I serve. Amen.

"You make known to me the path of life; in your presence there is fullness of joy; at your right hand are pleasures forevermore." (Psalm 16:11)

"Teaching them to observe all that I have commanded you. And behold, I am with you always, to the end of the age." (Matthew 28:20)

"In the cover of your presence you hide them from the plots of men; you store them in your shelter from the strife of tongues." (Psalm 31:20)

"And I saw the holy city, new Jerusalem, coming down out of heaven from God, prepared as a bride adorned for her husband. And I heard a loud voice from the throne saying, 'Behold, the dwelling place of God is with man. He will dwell with them, and they will be his people, and God himself will be with them as their God. He will wipe away every tear from their eyes, and death shall be no more, neither shall there be mourning, nor crying, nor pain anymore, for the former things have passed away.'" (Revelation 21:2-4)

DAY 17
MY MORNING PRAYER

_____

_____

_____

_____

_____

_____

_____

_____

_____

_____

_____

_____

_____

_____

_____

_____

_____

DAY 17
EVENING PRAYER

I bless your Holy name, dear God. Grace and peace unto you, for you are the author and finisher of my faith. Thank you for saving me through the day. You have blessed me to survive another day. You have guided my footsteps, and you have shown me what to do. Thank you for allowing me to be obedient, to do what is pleasing in your sight, and let your blessings continue to pour upon me. In Jesus' name, Amen.

"For God so loved the world, that he gave his only Son, that whoever believes in him should not perish but have eternal life." (John 3:16)

"I can do all things through him who strengthens me." (Philippians 4:13)

"These are grumblers, malcontents, following their own sinful desires; they are loud-mouthed boasters, showing favoritism to gain advantage." (Jude 1:16)

DAY 17
MY EVENING PRAYER

_____

_____

_____

_____

_____

_____

_____

_____

_____

_____

_____

_____

_____

_____

_____

_____

_____

_____

DAY 18
MORNING PRAYER

Lord of hosts, thank you for waking me up this morning. I bless your holy name. You have given me another day to survive and to do the work that you want me to do.

Go before me and guide my path. Show me what to do so that I can do the things that are pleasing in your sight, and grant me the mercy to endure all that is before me.

I bless your holy name. Help me to run this race to be like you, and to not sin against you. Thank you once again for giving me the strength.

In Jesus' name, Amen.

DAY 18
MY MORNING PRAYER

_____

_____

_____

_____

_____

_____

_____

_____

_____

_____

_____

_____

_____

_____

_____

_____

_____

_____

_____

DAY 18
EVENING PRAYER

Lord, when my heart is overwhelmed with joy, I magnify you this evening. You have blessed me to survive another day, and I am overwhelmed with your peace and joy as you lead me the way you want me. You are my rock and my salvation. Thank you for the open doors of opportunity, both seen and unseen. Grant me the courage to step through those doors with faith and confidence. In Jesus' name, Amen.

"Fear not, for I am with you; be not dismayed, for I am your God; I will strengthen you, I will help you, I will uphold you with my righteous right hand." (Isaiah 41:10)

"Your word is a lamp to my feet and a light to my path." (Psalm 119:105)

"Do your best to present yourself to God as one approved, a worker who has no need to be ashamed, rightly handling the word of truth." (2 Timothy 2:15)

DAY 18
MY EVENING PRAYER

_____

_____

_____

_____

_____

_____

_____

_____

_____

_____

_____

_____

_____

_____

_____

_____

_____

_____

DAY 19
MORNING PRAYER

Lord, I seek success, not solely for my own gain but for the greater good. May the work of my hands be a source of blessing to others and a reflection of your grace. Open doors for me to be a source of joy and encouragement to those I meet. In Jesus' name, Amen.

"Commit your work to the LORD, and your plans will be established." (Proverbs 16:3)

"I can do all things through him who strengthens me." (Philippians 4:13)

"Delight yourself in the LORD, and he will give you the desires of your heart." (Psalm 37:4)

"My son, do not forget my teaching, but let your heart keep my commandments, for length of days and years of life and peace they will add to you. Let not steadfast love and faithfulness forsake you; bind them around your neck; write them on the tablet of your heart. So you will find favor and good success in the sight of God and man." (Proverbs 3:1-4)

"Humble yourselves before the Lord, and he will exalt you." (James 4:10)

DAY 19
MY MORNING PRAYER

_____

_____

_____

_____

_____

_____

_____

_____

_____

_____

_____

_____

_____

_____

_____

_____

_____

_____

DAY 19
EVENING PRAYER

Father, thank you for today, for all the ways in which I have known you. Thank you for covering me this day. May my dreaming be of you always and your direction. Lord, I ask you to bless me and give a long, healthy, and wealthy life. Give me the strength to endure all that I am facing. I bless your holy name, and I know you will never leave me nor forsake me. You said knock and the door will be open for me, so now, Lord, I am knocking at your door through prayer. Thank you for your blessing, thank you for your grace. In Jesus' name, Amen.

"If you lie down, you will not be afraid; when you lie down, your sleep will be sweet." (Proverbs 3:24)

"Sweet is the sleep of a laborer, whether he eats little or much, but the full stomach of the rich will not let him sleep." (Ecclesiastes 5:12)

"For God so loved the world, that he gave his only Son, that whoever believes in him should not perish but have eternal life." (John 3:16)

"For to us a child is born, to us a son is given; and the government shall be upon his shoulder, and his name shall be called Wonderful Counselor, Mighty God, Everlasting Father, Prince of Peace." (Isaiah 9:6)

DAY 19
MY EVENING PRAYER

_____

_____

_____

_____

_____

_____

_____

_____

_____

_____

_____

_____

_____

_____

_____

_____

_____

DAY 20
MORNING PRAYER

Fill my heart with your peace, your love, and your joy, so that I may radiate your presence to everyone I encounter today. May this day be a testament to your faithfulness and a step toward the purpose you have for my life. In the name of Jesus, I pray. Amen.

"Keep your heart with all vigilance, for from it flow the springs of life." (Proverbs 4:23)

"Create in me a clean heart, O God, and renew a right spirit within me." (Psalm 51:10)

"And I will give you a new heart, and a new spirit I will put within you. And I will remove the heart of stone from your flesh and give you a heart of flesh." (Ezekiel 36:26)

"Trust in the LORD with all your heart, and do not lean on your own understanding. In all your ways acknowledge him, and he will make straight your paths." (Proverbs 3:5-6)

DAY 20
MYMORNING PRAYER

_____

_____

_____

_____

_____

_____

_____

_____

_____

_____

_____

_____

_____

_____

_____

_____

_____

_____

_____

_____

DAY 20
EVENING PRAYER

Now I wake this morning, I bless your holy name. Thank you for keeping me through the night and watching over me, for you are my God and savior. Grant mercy on my soul, oh God, and carry me through everything that I have to do as you walk alongside me. Keep me safe through the night, Lord, for there is no one but you to guide and protect me. In Jesus' name, Amen.

"Keep your heart with all vigilance, for from it flow the springs of life." (Proverbs 4:23)

"Create in me a clean heart, O God, and renew a right spirit within me." (Psalm 51:10)

"And I will give you a new heart, and a new spirit I will put within you. And I will remove the heart of stone from your flesh and give you a heart of flesh." (Ezekiel 36:26)

"Trust in the LORD with all your heart, and do not lean on your own understanding. In all your ways acknowledge him, and he will make straight your paths." (Proverbs 3:5-6)

DAY 20
MY EVENING PRAYER

_____

_____

_____

_____

_____

_____

_____

_____

_____

_____

_____

_____

_____

_____

_____

_____

_____

DAY 21
MORNING PAYER

O God, you have woken me up this morning, and I thank you for waking me up today. Strengthen me so that I can go about this day, as you place the cloth of righteousness on me. I praise your holy name, and even though the day may be dark, you will bring light in my path so that I can see clearly in my walking with you. I am placing my hope and trust in you and am forever grateful, for you are the source of my life. In Jesus' name, Amen.

"May the God of hope fill you with all joy and peace in believing, so that by the power of the Holy Spirit you may abound in hope." (Romans 15:13)

"For I know the plans I have for you, declares the LORD, plans for welfare and not for evil, to give you a future and a hope." (Jeremiah 29:11)

"But they who wait for the LORD shall renew their strength; they shall mount up with wings like eagles; they shall run and not be weary; they shall walk and not faint." (Isaiah 40:31)

"Now faith is the assurance of things hoped for, the conviction of things not seen." (Hebrews 11:1)

DAY 21
MY MORNING PRAYER

_____

_____

_____

_____

_____

_____

_____

_____

_____

_____

_____

_____

_____

_____

_____

_____

_____

_____

DAY 21
EVENING PRAYER

Now, I lay me down to rest. I am thanking you, my Lord, for you are my life and my savior, and I bless your holy name. Thank you for filling my day with joy and peace. Thank you for going before me in spirit and in truth so that I can function accordingly. Let me wake and see another day, Lord. In Jesus' name, Amen.

"Blessed is the man who trusts in the LORD, whose trust is the LORD." (Jeremiah 17:7)

"Blessed are the poor in spirit, for theirs is the kingdom of heaven. Blessed are those who mourn, for they shall be comforted. Blessed are the meek, for they shall inherit the earth. Blessed are those who hunger and thirst for righteousness, for they shall be satisfied." (Matthew 5:3-6)

"Blessed is he who comes in the name of the LORD! We bless you from the house of the LORD." (Psalm 118:26)

"Blessed is the man who walks not in the

counsel of the wicked, nor stands in the way of sinners, nor sits in the seat of scoffers." (Psalm 1:1)

"Blessed are the pure in heart, for they shall see God. Blessed are the peacemakers, for they shall be called sons of God. Blessed are those who are persecuted for righteousness' sake, for theirs is the kingdom of heaven. Blessed are you when others revile you and persecute you and utter all kinds of evil against you falsely on my account. Rejoice and be glad, for your reward is great in heaven, for so they persecuted the prophets who were before you." (Matthew 5:8-12)

DAY 21
MY EVENING PRAYER

_____

_____

_____

_____

_____

_____

_____

_____

_____

_____

_____

_____

_____

_____

_____

_____

_____

_____

DAY 22
MORNING PRAYER

Lord, I thank you. Lord, I praise your holy name. I wake to see another day. Help me through the trials and tribulations that I may meet. Walk before me and order my steps, Lord. Allow me to face all situations, grant me the favors that I seek from you, and allow me to humble myself in every way possible. Strengthen me and guide me through the challenges of this new day. In Jesus' name, Amen.

"I can do all things through him who strengthens me." (Philippians 4:13)

"Fear not, for I am with you; be not dismayed, for I am your God; I will strengthen you, I will help you, I will uphold you with my righteous right hand." (Isaiah 41:10)

"But they who wait for the LORD shall renew their strength; they shall mount up with wings like eagles; they shall run and not be weary; they shall walk and not faint." (Isaiah 40:31)

"Finally, be strong in the Lord and in the strength of his might." (Ephesians 6:10)

DAY 22
MY MORNING PRAYER

DAY 22
MY EVENING PRAYER

Heavenly Father I bless your Holy name. You have blessed this day for me so that I can return home. I thank you and praise your home. You are the author and finisher for my faith. You have shown me what to do to, and I thank you for giving me the strength to be obedient to your word. Help me to understand more of your teaching, and please give we the boldness to serve you, and to tell others about you.

You have blessed me this day and all that I ask is that you forgive me of my sins and shortcoming, so that I can worship you always.

Help me to have a good night sleep, so that I can continue to serve you tomorrow.

In Jesus name Amen

[24]"The LORD bless you, and keep you; [25]the LORD make his face shine on you and be gracious to you; [26]the LORD turn his face toward you and give you peace.'"

Numbers 6:24-26

And my God will supply every need of yours according to his riches in glory in Christ Jesus. Philippians 4:19

Every good gift and every perfect gift is from above, coming down from the Father of lights with whom there is no variation or shadow due to change. James 1:17

Give, and it will be given to you. Good measure, pressed down, shaken together, running over, will be put into your lap. For with the measure you use it will be measured back to you." Luke 6:38

The Lord bless you and keep you; the Lord make his face to shine upon you and be gracious to you; the Lord lift up his countenance upon you and give you peace.

Numbers 6:24-26

Fear not, for I am with you; be not dismayed, for I am your God; I will strengthen you, I will help you, I will uphold you with my righteous right hand. Isaiah 41:10

Beloved, I pray that all may go well with you and that you may be in good health, as it goes well with your soul. 3 John 1:2

DAY 2
EVENING PRAYER

_____

_____

_____

_____

_____

_____

_____

_____

_____

_____

_____

_____

_____

_____

_____

_____

_____

_____

DAY 23
MORNING PRAYER

Father, praise be unto you. You are my God. Bless me as I go through the day. Thank you for reminding me that life is not always easy, but that we don't have to carry the hard into each new day.

Forgive me for dwelling on the past and for holding onto grudges, and bless my heart to be held back by nothing as we seek you each day. In Jesus' name, Amen.

"For if you forgive others their trespasses, your heavenly Father will also forgive you, but if you do not forgive others their trespasses, neither will your Father forgive your trespasses." (Matthew 6:14-15)

"Let all bitterness and wrath and anger and clamor and slander be put away from you, along with all malice. Be kind to one another, tenderhearted, forgiving one another, as God in Christ forgave you." (Ephesians 4:31-32)

"If we confess our sins, he is faithful and just to forgive us our sins and to cleanse us from all unrighteousness." (1 John 1:9)

"And whenever you stand praying, forgive, if you have anything against anyone, so that your Father also who is in heaven may forgive you your trespasses." (Mark 11:25)

DAY 23
MY MORNING PRAYER

_____

_____

_____

_____

_____

_____

_____

_____

_____

_____

_____

_____

_____

_____

_____

_____

_____

DAY 23
MY EVENING PRAYER

Thank you, God, for today. Thank you for blessing me. Thank you, God, for guiding, sustaining, and granting us the spiritual, physical, and emotional strength to get through each day. Give me the strength to continue another day so that I can live a peaceful life. You are the God that I serve and the God whom I love and cherish. Grant me mercy, and allow me to grow the way you want me to be, for there is no one like you. In Jesus' name, Amen.

"There is therefore now no condemnation for those who are in Christ Jesus." (Romans 8:1)

"So God created man in his own image, in the image of God he created him; male and female he created them." (Genesis 1:27)

"Let no one say when he is tempted, 'I am being tempted by God,' for God cannot be tempted with evil, and he himself tempts no one. But each person is tempted when he is lured and enticed by his own desire." (James 1:13-14)

DAY 23
MY EVENING PRAYER

_____

_____

_____

_____

_____

_____

_____

_____

_____

_____

_____

_____

_____

_____

_____

_____

_____

DAY 24
MORNING PRAYERS

Dear Lord, this is the day that you have made. Let your blessings continue to flow as you open my eyes this morning. Thank you for waking me up and thank you for blessing me with the gift of life this morning. Guide my footsteps, Lord, and continue guiding me in the direction that you have given me. Give me strength today to be strong for you, and thank you in advance for carrying me when I am too weak. If I stumble into temptation, forgive me, and lead me away from them, for I need your strength to overcome everything that is not pleasing in your sight. In Jesus' name, Amen.

"For if you forgive others their trespasses, your heavenly Father will also forgive you, but if you do not forgive others their trespasses, neither will your Father forgive your trespasses." (Matthew 6:14-15)

"Let all bitterness and wrath and anger and clamor and slander be put away from you, along with all malice. Be kind to one another, tenderhearted, forgiving one another, as God in Christ forgave you." (Ephesians 4:31-32)

"If we confess our sins, he is faithful and just to forgive us our sins and to cleanse us from all unrighteousness." (1 John 1:9)

DAY 24
MY MORNING PRAYER

_____

_____

_____

_____

_____

_____

_____

_____

_____

_____

_____

_____

_____

_____

_____

_____

_____

_____

_____

DAY 24
MY EVENING PRAYER

Heavenly Father you know what's on my heart, and you know what's on my mind, and you knew my desire even before I ask of you. I am praising your name for you are the guiding force of my life, and I thank you.

I am looking forward for tomorrow and ask that you would be ahead of me in everything that I do and say. Please help me to make prayerful decisions that will bring glory and honor to you, and I ask that you watch over me and keep me safe wherever I go.

Forgive me for my sins and short coming, and help me make prayerful decisions that will bring glory to You always.

In Jesus Name Amen

For I know the plans I have for you, declares the Lord, plans to prosper you and not to harm you, plans to give you hope and a future. Jeremiah 29:11

And my God will meet all your needs according to the riches of his glory in Christ Jesus. Philippians 4:19

Worship the Lord your God, and his blessing will be on your food and water. I will take away sickness from among you. Exodus 23:25

DAY 24
MY EVENING PRAYER

_____

_____

_____

_____

_____

_____

_____

_____

_____

_____

_____

_____

_____

_____

_____

_____

_____

_____

Thank you for blessing me. Thank you for waking me up today. Let your Holy Spirit flow. When I triumph against challenges, I praise you, Father. Without you, I would not have life nor the strength to live. Bless my loved ones with the strength you have given me, Lord. You are worthy of all praise and worship. You are my strength and my protection. In Jesus' name, Amen.

"I can do all things through him who strengthens me." (Philippians 4:13)

"Fear not, for I am with you; be not dismayed, for I am your God; I will strengthen you, I will help you, I will uphold you with my righteous right hand." (Isaiah 41:10)

"But they who wait for the LORD shall renew their strength; they shall mount up with wings like eagles; they shall run and not be weary; they shall walk and not faint." (Isaiah 40:31)

"Finally, be strong in the Lord and in the strength of his might." (Ephesians 6:10)

"My flesh and my heart may fail, but God is the strength of my heart and my portion forever." (Psalm 73:26)

DAY 25
MY MORNING PRAYER

_____

_____

_____

_____

_____

_____

_____

_____

_____

_____

_____

_____

_____

_____

_____

_____

_____

_____

DAY 25
EVENING PRAYER

Blessed be the name of the Lord, for you are worthy to be praised. Once again, you have blessed me with the gift of life, and I am grateful. No words can explain how I feel. I am filled with joy because I know of your love for me. I am praising your name and glorifying you. Thank you, Jesus, for your blessing. Thank you, Jesus, for your kindness. Thank you, Jesus, for giving me life. Fill me with your Holy Spirit. Give me the strength to endure. In Jesus' name, Amen.

"For his disciples had gone away into the city to buy food. The Samaritan woman said to him, 'How is it that you, a Jew, ask for a drink from me, a woman of Samaria?' (For Jews have no dealings with Samaritans.)" (John 4:8-9)

"Son of man, raise a lamentation over the king of Tyre, and say to him, Thus says the Lord GOD: 'You were the signet of perfection, full of wisdom and perfect in beauty. You were in Eden, the garden of God; every precious stone was your covering, sardius, topaz, and diamond, beryl, onyx, and jasper, sapphire, emerald, and carbuncle; and crafted in gold were your settings and your engravings. On the day that you were created they were prepared. You were an anointed guardian cherub. I placed you; you were on the holy mountain of God; in the midst of the stones of fire you walked. You were blameless in your ways from the day you were created, till unrighteousness was found in you.'" (Ezekiel 28:12-15)

DAY 25
MY EVENING PRAYER

_____

_____

_____

_____

_____

_____

_____

_____

_____

_____

_____

_____

_____

_____

_____

_____

_____

_____

Blessed be the name of the Lord, for you are worthy to be praised. Once again, you have blessed me with the gift of life, and I am grateful. No words can explain how I feel. I am filled with joy because I know of your love for me. I am praising your name and glorifying you. Thank you, Jesus, for your blessing. Thank you, Jesus, for your kindness. Thank you, Jesus, for giving me life. Fill me with your Holy Spirit. Give me the strength to endure. In Jesus' name, Amen.

"For his disciples had gone away into the city to buy food. The Samaritan woman said to him, 'How is it that you, a Jew, ask for a drink from mc, a woman of Samaria?' (For Jews have no dealings with Samaritans.)" (John 4:8-9)

"Son of man, raise a lamentation over the king of Tyre, and say to him, Thus says the Lord GOD: 'You were the signet of perfection, full of wisdom and perfect in beauty. You were in Eden, the garden of God; every precious stone was your covering, sardius, topaz, and diamond, beryl, onyx, and jasper, sapphire, emerald, and carbuncle; and crafted in gold were your settings and your engravings. On the day that you were created they were prepared. You were an anointed guardian cherub. I placed you; you were on the holy mountain of God; in the midst of the stones of fire you walked. You were blameless in your ways from the day you were created, till unrighteousness was found in you.'" (Ezekiel 28:12-15)

DAY 26
MY MORNING PRAYER

_____

_____

_____

_____

_____

_____

_____

_____

_____

_____

_____

_____

_____

_____

_____

_____

_____

_____

_____

DAY 26
EVENING PRAYER

Heaving Father I am your servant. I am your child, You have paved the way for me today. You have blessed me to get through another day. I worship and adore you because you are a father who is true to your word. You have shown me daily how wonderful you are to me. You have blessed my family, you are walking along side me daily, and I am very grateful.

Thank you for allowing me not to be discourage, but to follow you, I am praising your name today and always.

I believe that you are working in my flife evn whe I don't feel it. Thank you for allowing me to call your name even when I am not worthy.

I bless your Holy name, and thank you for covering me always.

In Jusus name Amen.

The Lord bless you and keep you; the Lord make his face shine on you and be gracious to you; the Lord turn his face toward you and give you peace. Numbers 6:24-26

But blessed is the one who trusts in the Lord, whose confidence is in him.

They will be like a tree planted by the water that sends out its roots by the stream. It does not fear when heat comes; its leaves are always green.

It has no worries in a year of drought and never fails to bear fruit. Jeremiah 17:7-8

DAY 26
MY EVENING PRAYER

_____

_____

_____

_____

_____

_____

_____

_____

_____

_____

_____

_____

_____

_____

_____

_____

_____

_____

DAY 27
MORNING PRAYERS

Blessing, oh God, for you are merciful to me. Thank you for giving me the strength to wake up and see another day. I praise your name and seek you for strength and guidance. Help me to live the life that you want me to live, and help me to walk in alignment with you daily. Go before me in every step that I take. Today is another day that you have blessed me with, and I am grateful for bringing me through so that I can serve you. I praise your name and ask that you have mercy upon my soul not only for this day but always. In Jesus' name, I pray. Amen.

"The fear of the LORD is the beginning of knowledge; fools despise wisdom and instruction." (Proverbs 1:7)

"An intelligent heart acquires knowledge, and the ear of the wise seeks knowledge." (Proverbs 18:15)

"For the LORD gives wisdom; from his mouth come knowledge and understanding." (Proverbs 2:6)

"Whoever loves discipline loves knowledge, but he who hates reproof is stupid." (Proverbs 12:1)

"The fear of the LORD is the beginning of wisdom, and knowledge of the Holy One is understanding." (Proverbs 9:10)

DAY 27
MY MORNING PRAYER

_____

_____

_____

_____

_____

_____

_____

_____

_____

_____

_____

_____

_____

_____

_____

_____

_____

_____

_____

DAY 27
EVENING PRAYER

Heavenly Father, up above, please bless me this night. Let me sleep all through the night and grant me peace. You are my God and the Lord who protects me, guides me, and points me in the right direction. Let my night and my dreams be pure delight. You know my heart and desire, and I thank you for your blessing. Thank you for your love. In Jesus' name, Amen.

"Delight yourself in the LORD, and he will give you the desires of your heart." (Psalm 37:4)

"But the meek shall inherit the land and delight themselves in abundant peace." (Psalm 37:11)

"If you return to the Almighty, you will be built up; if you remove injustice far from your tents, if you lay gold in the dust, and gold of Ophir among the stones of the torrent-bed, then the Almighty will be your gold and your precious silver. For then you will delight yourself in the Almighty and lift up your face to God." (Job 22:23-26)

"But his delight is in the law of the LORD, and on his law he meditates day and night." (Psalm 1:2)

DAY 27
MY EVENING PRAYER

_____
_____
_____
_____
_____
_____
_____
_____
_____
_____
_____
_____
_____
_____
_____
_____
_____
_____

DAY 28
MORNING PRAYER

Heavenly Father, please cleanse my thoughts of anger and worry. I know that worry is not your will for me. Please provide for all my needs as you promise in your word. I give to you all my fears, cares, and troubles, as you have told me to do. Bring peace and comfort to my heart and help me to rest in you and have peace. Forgive me for any sins that I have committed today and fill my heart with your love. In Jesus' name, Amen.

"Blessed be the God and Father of our Lord Jesus Christ, the Father of mercies and God of all comfort, who comforts us in all our affliction, so that we may be able to comfort those who are in any affliction, with the comfort with which we ourselves are comforted by God." (2 Corinthians 1:3-4)

"Even though I walk through the valley of the shadow of death, I will fear no evil, for you are with me; your rod and your staff, they comfort me." (Psalm 23:4)

"Come to me, all who labor and are heavy laden, and I will give you rest. Take my yoke upon you, and learn from me, for I am gentle and lowly in heart, and you will find rest for your souls. For my yoke is easy, and my burden is light." (Matthew 11:28-30)

DAY 28
MY MORNING PRAYER

_____

_____

_____

_____

_____

_____

_____

_____

_____

_____

_____

_____

_____

_____

_____

_____

_____

DAY 28
EVENING PRAYER

Oh Lord, as I close my eyes tonight, I want to thank you for your boundless love that surrounds me always, for your love is a constant source of comfort and assurance in my life. Help me to truly feel and experience your love in the quiet moments of the night. Let your love wash over me, soothing any worries or anxieties, and fill my heart with the warmth of your presence.

Thank you for loving me unconditionally, for knowing me completely, and for always being there for me. I am grateful for your love, and I cherish the relationship I have with you. As I sleep, may I rest in the assurance of your love, knowing that you are watching over me and guiding me.

In Jesus' name, I pray. Amen.

"Again, if two lie together, they keep warm, but how can one keep warm alone?" (Ecclesiastes 4:11)

"For God so loved the world, that he gave his only Son, that whoever believes in him should not perish but have eternal life." (John 3:16)

"Again I will build you, and you shall be built, O virgin Israel! Again you shall adorn yourself with tambourines and shall go forth in the dance of the merrymakers." (Jeremiah 31:4)

DAY 28
MY EVENING PRAYER

_____

_____

_____

_____

_____

_____

_____

_____

_____

_____

_____

_____

_____

_____

_____

_____

_____

DAY 29
MORNING PRAYERS

Lord God Almighty, we pray for your great mercy, that you guide us towards you. Guide us to your will, to the need of our soul, for we cannot do it ourselves. Make our minds steadfast in your will and aware of our soul's need. Strengthen us against the temptations of the devil, remove from us all lust and every unrighteousness, and shield us against our foes, seen and unseen. Teach us to do your will, that we may inwardly love you before all things with a pure mind. For you are our maker and our redeemer, our help, our comfort, our trust, and our hope. Praise and glory be to you now and forever. Amen.

"But now that you have been set free from sin and have become slaves of God, the fruit you get leads to sanctification and its end, eternal life." (Romans 6:22)

"Who gave himself for us to redeem us from all lawlessness and to purify for himself a people for his own possession who are zealous for good works." (Titus 2:14)

"I have blotted out your transgressions like a cloud and your sins like mist; return to me, for I have redeemed you." (Isaiah 44:22)

DAY 29
MY MORNING PRAYER

_____

_____

_____

_____

_____

_____

_____

_____

_____

_____

_____

_____

_____

_____

_____

_____

_____

_____

DAY 29
EVENING PRAYER

O Lord, enlighten our hearts by your holy radiance, Jesus Christ, that we may serve you without fear in holiness and righteousness all the days of our life. In Him, may we survive the storms of this world, and by His guidance reach the country of eternal brightness; through your mercy, O blessed Lord, you live and govern all things, now and forever. In Jesus' name, Amen.

"Strive for peace with everyone, and for the holiness without which no one will see the Lord." (Hebrews 12:14)

"Since we have these promises, beloved, let us cleanse ourselves from every defilement of body and spirit, bringing holiness to completion in the fear of God." (2 Corinthians 7:1)

"But you are a chosen race, a royal priesthood, a holy nation, a people for his own possession, that you may proclaim the excellencies of him who called you out of darkness into his marvelous light." (1 Peter 2:9)

"But as he who called you is holy, you also be holy in all your conduct." (1 Peter 1:15-16)

29
MY EVENING PRAYER

_____

_____

_____

_____

_____

_____

_____

_____

_____

_____

_____

_____

_____

_____

_____

_____

_____

_____

Oh Lord and Savior, thank you for this new day and the breath of life within me that you have given to me. I am grateful for your steadfast love and kindness, and the blessings surrounding me. As I step out into the world today, guide, protect, and fill my heart with gratitude and joy. May my actions reflect your grandeur and bring glory to your name.

"No weapon that is fashioned against you shall succeed, and you shall refute every tongue that rises against you in judgment. This is the heritage of the servants of the LORD and their vindication from me, declares the LORD." (Isaiah 54:17)

"God is our refuge and strength, a very present help in trouble." (Psalm 46:1)

"Fear not, for I am with you; be not dismayed, for I am your God; I will strengthen you, I will help you, I will uphold you with my righteous right hand." (Isaiah 41:10)

"Beloved, never avenge yourselves, but leave it to the wrath of God, for it is written,

'Vengeance is mine, I will repay, says the Lord.'" (Romans 12:19)

"You are a hiding place for me; you preserve me from trouble; you surround me with shouts of deliverance." (Psalm 32:7)

DAY 30
MY MORNING PRAYER

_____

_____

_____

_____

_____

_____

_____

_____

_____

_____

_____

_____

_____

_____

_____

_____

_____

DAY 30
EVENING PRAYER

Lord, I want to give you the glory that belongs to you, for you are the author and finisher of my faith. Please, God, continue to grant mercy on me. You are everything to me, Lord. Thank you for your mercy and grace, and for your goodness. Thank you for being you. In Jesus' name, Amen.

"Know, then, that the Lord, your God, is God: the faithful God who keeps covenant mercy to the thousandth generation toward those who love him and keep his commandments." (Deuteronomy 7:9)

"All the paths of the Lord are mercy and truth toward those who honor his covenant and decrees." (Psalm 25:10)

"No one who conceals transgressions will prosper, but one who confesses and forsakes them will obtain mercy." (Proverbs 28:13)

"Therefore the Lord waits to be gracious to you; therefore he will rise up to show mercy to you. For the Lord is a God of justice; blessed are all those who wait for him." (Isaiah 30:18)

"The steadfast love of the Lord never ceases, his mercies never come to an end; they are new every morning; great is your faithfulness." (Lamentations 3:22-23)

DAY 30
MY EVENING PRAYER

_____

_____

_____

_____

_____

_____

_____

_____

_____

_____

_____

_____

_____

_____

_____

_____

_____

_____

DAY 31
MORNING PRYER

Heavenly Father, you meet me as I start this day and open my eyes, and with gratitude, I am blessing your holy name today. Thank you for this gift of life and for the opportunities that you will give to me. I am asking that you guide my steps and my thoughts today. Help me to walk in your light and to make the right choices so that I can honor you and reflect your love not only today but always.

Give me wisdom to make smart decisions and the strength to face any challenges that may arise, and fill me with your peace, love, and joy so that I can help those around me. In Jesus' name, Amen.

"Commit to the Lord whatever you do, and he will establish your plans." (Proverbs 16:3)

"For I know the plans I have for you, declares the Lord, plans to prosper you and not to harm you, plans to give you hope and a future." (Jeremiah 29:11)

"And my God will meet all your needs according to the riches of his glory in Christ Jesus." (Philippians 4:19)

DAY 31
MY MORNING PRAYER

_____

_____

_____

_____

_____

_____

_____

_____

_____

_____

_____

_____

_____

_____

_____

_____

_____

_____

DAY 31
EVENING PRAYER

Gracious God, as I prepare to go to bed, I bless your holy name. I lay before you the events of this day, and ask for forgiveness of my sins and shortcomings. Let your mercy cover me. Grant me a restful sleep and surround me with your protective presence. May your angels watch over me and my family. Thank you for being my refuge, for your grace, and your goodness throughout this day. Even though I am not worthy to call your name, thank you for all that you do, and please fill my dreams with your peace. In Jesus' name, Amen.

"But you, O Lord, are a shield about me, my glory, and the lifter of my head. I cried aloud to the Lord, and he answered me from his holy hill. Selah. I lay down and slept; I woke again, for the Lord sustained me." (Psalm 3:3-5)

"You have put more joy in my heart than they have when their grain and wine abound. In peace I will both lie down and sleep; for

you alone, O Lord, make me dwell in safety."
(Psalm 4:7-8)

"The LORD commands his mercy during the day, and at night his song is with me—a prayer to the God of my life." (Psalm 42:8)

"When you lie down, you will not be afraid. As you lie there, your sleep will be sweet. Do not be afraid of sudden terror or of the destruction of wicked people when it comes. The LORD will be your confidence. He will keep your foot from getting caught." (Proverbs 3:24-26)

DAY 31
MY EVENING PRAYER

_____

_____

_____

_____

_____

_____

_____

_____

_____

_____

_____

_____

_____

_____

_____

_____

_____

_____

CONCLUSION

We must always remember that God answers prayers in His own time, not according to man's timing, and we must be willing to accept whatever the answer is, and do so with a clean heart, for there is a valid reason for His answers. He is a loving God and will never leave us or forsake us, and we must always trust Him.

We must recognize His voice because He speaks to us always. If we do not recognize it, we will miss our blessings. You must submit your life totally to Christ so that He can work through you.

For the Bible tells us, "Now this is the confidence that we have in Him, that if we ask anything according to His will, He hears us. And if we know that He hears us, whatever we ask, we know that we have the petitions that we have asked of Him." (1 John 5:14-15)

REFERENCES

Holy Bible

Bible Dictionary

Understanding the Purpose and Power of Prayer - Myles Munroe

Billy Graham Evangelistic Association:
https://billygraham.org/story/who-is-jesus

The Priority of Prayer – Dr. Charles Stanley

www.ingramcontent.com/pod-product-compliance
Lightning Source LLC
Chambersburg PA
CBHW071746120626
46550CB00002B/681